Gifts of God

Patricia Swift

Deerfield Beach, FL

Material from <u>Understanding the Bible</u> by Stephen L. Harris used by permission.

The U.S.A. map of the provinces of TEC used by permission from Morehouse Pub. Co.

Order this book online at www.trafford.com
or email orders@trafford.com

Most Trafford titles are also available at major online book retailers.

Note for Librarians: A cataloguing record for this book is available from Library and Archives Canada at www.collectionscanada.ca/amicus/index-e.html

Printed in Victoria, BC, Canada.

ISBN: 978-1-4269-1773-8

Our mission is to efficiently provide the world's finest, most comprehensive book publishing service, enabling every author to experience success. To find out how to publish your book, your way, and have it available worldwide, visit us online at www.trafford.com

Trafford rev. 9/3/2009

 www.trafford.com

North America & international
toll-free: 1 888 232 4444 (USA & Canada)
phone: 250 383 6864 ♦ fax: 812 355 4082

Table of Contents

Assignment

Preview

Focus God's Story

Focus Gifts of Calls

Focus The Old Testament

Insight

Review

Activities

APPENDIXES

BIBLIOGRAPHY

1
The Gift of Scriptures
Old Testament

ASSIGNMENT

Gen 1: 27-28

Ps 8: 3-8

Gen 12: 1-3

Gen 15: 18-21

Gen 17: 5-8

Gen 32: 28

Gen 46: 1-3

Num 23: 21-23

Exod 3: 1-10

Exod 20: 1-17

Exod 24: 3-8

Isa 11: 1-9

2 Sam 2: 4

2 Sam 7: 8-17

Ps 89: 3, 19-37

Jer 31: 31-34

PREVIEW

This session of the gift of Scriptures includes God's creation and mankind's role. It considers God as ruler saving mankind from evil. In the selected passages we hear God's call to Abraham, to Moses, and to David, and we see the related gifts. In addition, we look briefly at the rest of the collected books of the Old Testament.

FOCUS: GOD'S STORY

There is real risk in shortening God's story to only seven short chapters. Why? These gifts are but an early prologue to an infinite number of chapters in God's story. That story continues within each of us this day.

The Old Testament (OT) of the Holy Bible presents anything but a straightforward story in its thirty-nine books. Rather, it is a multi-faceted collection of law, prophecy, history, myth, fiction, drama, poetry, legend and wisdom.

Themes abound in the OT. For example, a reader finds sin, judgment, redemption, kingdom, shepherd, call and covenant. In spite of thematic abundance, a listener hears God creating and clarifying the role of mankind. A listener hears, too, God as ruler who saves us from evil.

FOCUS GIFTS OF CALLS

Besides the overwhelming gift of creation, we hear God as he intervenes in human events to call or to name Abram, providing him in covenant with promises of land and progeny. We hear of Jacob and the twelve tribes of Israel as the chosen as they are saved from slavery in Egypt.

We hear God call Moses and the Ten Commandments that result. We also hear of God's special relationship with David in his covenant and the hope for a new David, a new Messiah, as well as the establishing of Government in Jerusalem. Gen. 9:1-17 narrates an account of Noah, called as the new father of mankind. The rainbow serves as a sign of the call. The sign accompanying both the covenant with Abraham and with David is circumcision.

God chooses to create and to intervene in history in covenants or special testaments with certain persons or groups. He created us because he desires that we worship him. OT worship consists of reciting God's mighty acts, his calls to covenant renewal, and our repentance for lack of faith.

The Psalms particularly reveal this worship. God has created people to serve him, to proclaim him, and to show knowledge of him. Governmental problems arise as mankind refuses to acknowledge just who it is who is in charge, in whose kingdom we live. Though God judges with wrath, his goodness prevails with our faith promising fulfillment through New Testament events.

FOCUS THE OLD TESTAMENT

The OT collection of books originally written mostly in Hebrew covers more than 2000 years of history. It exists in a number of translations in many languages. Scholars have identified J,E,D, and P as theoretical sources in the writing of the first five OT books (Jahweh, Elohist, Deuteronomist, and Priestly). Scholars first divided the OT into three groups of books: Law, Prophecy, and

Writings. The corresponding Hebrew words are Torah, Nevi'im,

and Kethuvim. In addition to the OT, the Apocrypha has 15 books

of intertestamental literature.

INSIGHT

In biblical calls God provides saving events for mankind. The calls

imply responses and gifts. Mankind's responses include treaties,

ties, and covenants initiated by God.

Berit, the Hebrew word for covenant, suggests a vow, a promise, a

contract, pact, or agreement. Covenants may carry some conditions

or no conditions. They may make demands or make no demands on

the recipient. The covenants with Abraham and David have "no

strings." That is, they impose no certain response. The covenant

with Moses, however, expects Israel to obey the commandments.

REVIEW

In the gifts of OT scriptures, then, themes of creation, kingdom, and calls dominate. The calls of persons come with covenants that may demand a response. The answers of Abraham, Moses, and David produce particular relationships with God. This oversimplification allows us some entry into OT times.

ACTIVITIES

Invite class members to list those persons called in covenant with God. Then construct on board (newsprint on easel) a box chart using words familiar to the class . For example, column headings could be person, promise, sign, and demand or condition. Another box chart could include the four documentary hypotheses: J, E, D, and P with writing style, approximate date, and supposed place of writing.

2
The Gift of
Scriptures
New Testament

ASSIGNMENT

1 Cor 11: 25	Lk 11: 1-4
Mk 14: 24-25	Mk 13: 32
Mt 26: 26-29	Jn 3: 1-5
2 Cor 3: 4-6	Mt 28: 16-20
Heb 8: 1-13	Acts 2: 38-42
Acts 13: 16-23	Acts 4: 29-31
Mt 1: 18-21	Jn 20: 19-23

Isa 42: 6	Acts 2: 1-11
Rom 3: 21-25a	Acts 1: 8
Heb 2: 14-17	Acts 1: 1-5
1 Jn 2: 1-2	Acts 6: 1-7
2 Cor 5: 18-19	Phil 2: 5-11
Mk 14: 25	Lk 22: 28-30
Mt 6: 9-15	Acts 5: 14-16
Acts 9: 10-15	Acts 14: 23
Acts 11: 11-18	Titus 1: 4-9

PREVIEW

This session considers in brief the New Covenant, Jesus' life, Christ as reconciliation, Paul's letters, the Kingdom, and the Church.

FOCUS NEW COVENANT

The New Covenant in Christ is of **faith or Spirit** rather than only obedience to Jewish law. Several names occur as metaphors for this covenant: new community of Israel, Abraham's progeny by faith, household of God, bride of Christ, heirs of the Kingdom, and company of the forgiven. Paul, Mark, and Matthew specify Jesus' blood as the New Covenant.

FOCUS JESUS CHRIST AS RECONCILIATION

Matthew and Luke, two of the four gospels of the NT, recount Jesus' birth, life, death, and resurrection. Mark, the earliest gospel, begins with Jesus' baptism. Jesus' advent or coming is a special intervention of God in history.

Jesus comes as fulfillment of promise. The NT reader learns of Jesus as expiation for our sins. This is his redeeming purpose: **to serve as our reconciliation with God. That is, to be again in union with God.** He reaches out to seek and save the lost.

FOCUS   PAUL'S LETTERS

"Therefore encourage one another and build up each other . . . ." (1 Thess 5: 11) (NRSV). Such exhortation might appear near the beginning of the NT if it were presented chronologically. Paul, author of this quotation and nearly one fourth of the NT receives too little attention. In a day enveloped by electronic mail, Paul still sends us readers many messages. Our Christian calendar recognizes his conversion January 25th and his sainthood, with Peter, June 29th, yet Paul offers guidelines for every day of the year.

Paul perseveres in spite of infirmity (2 Cor 12: 7-10). His conversion precedes his travel, preaching and missionary work for Christ. Arrested and imprisoned he continues to convey the good news.

Paul presents our first new covenant theology (2 Cor 3: 4-6, 1 Cor 11: 25). He provides us the oldest baptismal confession (Rom 1: 3-6), the earliest accounts of our Lord's Supper (1 Cor 11: 23-26) and Jesus' death and resurrection (1 Cor 15: 3-11).

Writing or dictating even before the author of Mark, the earliest gospel, Paul advises and chides groups of Thessalonians, Corinthians, Galations, Romans, and Philippians as well as those gathering in Philemon's house. From about 47 to 60 C.E. in journeys averaging two years each, he reaches many of these sites.

Of twenty-one NT books in letter form, seven, arranged by their length, seem genuinely Paul's. He authored neither the Pastorals of first and second Timothy and Titus nor Hebrews. Scholars still debate the authorship of 2 Thessalonians and Colossians.

In their usual format Paul's letters resemble our worship services with greeting, prayer and/or thanksgiving, body of advice or warning, personal messages, grace or benediction. They reach us readers with a hymn to love in 1 Cor 13 and knowledge of Jesus as reconciliation in 2 Cor 5: 14-21. These writings catalog vices in Rom 1: 28-32 and vices with virtues in Gal 5: 19-24. They tell us of spiritual gifts: Rom 6: 23, Rom 12: 6-8, Eph 2: 8 and 1 Cor 12:4-11. Paul can also be naughty (Gal 5: 12).

In his halting speech style, this saint tells us more than once to be constant in prayer (Rom: 12, 1 Thess 5: 17). He paradoxically sees into himself and us in our baseness: "I do not understand my own actions. For I do not do what I want, but I do the very thing I hate" (Rom 7: 15) (NRSV). This barely explores Paul's important correspondence with first century Christians and us.

FOCUS THE KINGDOM AND THE CHURCH

Jesus proclaims that God's time is fulfilled. As he is appointed,

Jesus appoints disciples. He teaches them to pray, "Thy Kingdom

come." When is the Kingdom coming? We believe complete ful-

fillment comes with Christ's return. We also believe we are already

part of the Kingdom here and now. Entry to the Kingdom is through

baptism.

Jesus tells the disciples to "make disciples of all nations" (Mt 28:

19), to baptize, and to teach. On Pentecost the Holy Spirit gives

special gifts of speech to his apostles. A variety of gifts comes to

each of us, and we, as the apostles, are told to pray in Jesus' name.

Jesus Christ is the Head of the Church. Passages from the Gospel

of John and the Book of Acts show us as successors to the OT

chosen in the New Israel. We learn, too, of the task of proclaiming

the gospel or good news and of early growth in numbers of apostles,

deacons,elders, and overseers. We can compare these with

deacons, priests, and bishops from the Greek words *deakonia,*

presbuteros, and episkopas.

FOCUS THE NEW TESTAMENT

The New Testament consists of 27 books originally written in Greek in a period of less than 100 years. In the gospels of Mark, Matthew, and Luke, the teachings of Jesus appear primarily in parables. These are puzzlements that, as Robert Capon says, include categories of Kingdom, grace, and judgment. In addition to the gospels and Acts, letters make up one third of the NT. The Book of Revelation envisions the present evil age and the coming age when God alone reigns.

INSIGHT

The term "testament" is a Latin translation of the Greek word "covenant." Expiation is an **atonement,** a making up for, a reparation for our sins as Jesus Christ gives himself for us. The Church is another name for the **Body of Christ**. We as followers of Christ are the Church gathered as we worship together and the Church scattered as we work, study, and play.

REVIEW

The New Covenant comes to us through Jesus. He serves us in his life, death, and resurrection as our reconciliation with God. We are already partially enjoying the Kingdom of God through Jesus Christ and his Body, the Church.

3 The Gift of the Body of Christ

ASSIGNMENT

Read and reflect on these passages: 1 Cor 12: 26-27; 1 Cor 12:   1;

Eph 4: 11-16.

PREVIEW

This session considers the church as the body of Christ, the

Episcopal Church, its seasons and symbols.

FOCUS THE BODY OF CHRIST

"The church is the body of Christ, a union of love, a oneness in Spirit, a life in common" (Westerhoff 13). Much as Abraham and Moses and David and Noah are called by God in covenant, **so are we called to be part of a continuation of Jesus Christ.**

Rather than a set of explicit instructions, Jesus Christ leaves us with his risen and ascended body within this fellowship of followers or disciples. John Westerhoff tells us that this church as the body of Christ is also a biblical and sacramental community. Michael Ramsey calls us "the people of God, the Israel of God, the ecclesia" (101). *Ecclesia* is the Greek word for our assembling with fellow believers.

How do we learn of this body of Christ, this covenant gathering? The Catechism or Outline of Faith in the Book of Common Prayer explains covenant. In the Old Testament of the Holy Bible covenant is given to the Hebrews by God. The Ten Commandments clearly show this contract or covenant. The commandments given to Moses teach us our "duty to God and our duty to our neighbors" (BCP 847).

The body of Christ has to do , too, with the Kingdom of God. In Luke 17.21 we read "the kingdom of God is among or within you." Even more pointed is <u>The Gospel of Thomas</u>: *"The kingdom is inside you and it is outside you."*

FOCUS THE EPISCOPAL CHURCH

The printed word allows us to leap from the first century to the eighteenth century. "Protestant Episcopal Church" was first used as a name in 1780. That term "protestant" meant *for* religious freedom as well as *against* Roman authority. In 1783 the full name was official: The Protestant Episcopal Church in the United States of America.

With offices of bishop, priest, and deacon the church considers the laity as essential in worship. After the Lambeth Conference of 1886, bishops established these principles of the Lambeth Quadrilateral:

1) **the Holy Scriptures, OT and NT as necessary to salvation;**

2) **The Apostles' Creed as Baptismal Symbol and the Nicene Creed as a sufficient statement of the Christian faith;**

3) **the two Sacraments ordained by Christ, Baptism and the Supper of the Lord; and**

4) **the Historic Episcopate to be adapted locally to needs of nations and peoples called to God in the Unity of His Church (BCP 877-878).**

In 1976 PECUSA officially became The Episcopal Church. While the Presbyterian Church has prebyters or elders as leaders, and the Congregational Church has its members in charge, the Episcopal Church has bishops in that role. Structurally our church is now divided into nine nongoverning provinces in this country.

In 2000 General Convention agreed to an alliance of the Episcopal Church and the Evangelical Lutheran Church in America (ELCA). This agreement allows full communion, sharing of liturgy and clergy with each denomination retaining its identity.

FOCUS SEASONS AND SYMBOLS

The seasons of the church can be divided into two cycles: incarnation and resurrection. The incarnation cycle includes Advent and Christmas through Epiphany. The resurrection cycle has Lent, Easter, Ascension, and Pentecost. These seasons benefit us greatly as we observe each interval in the life of our Lord each year.

Advent, preparation for the birth of Jesus Christ and his second coming in judgment;

Christmas, the birth of Jesus and the Incarnation;

Epiphany, manifestation, the coming of the magi January 6, Jesus' Baptism on the first Sunday after the Feast of the Epiphany, and the Transfiguration on the last Sunday;

Lent, repentance in preparation for Easter, 40 days

(excluding Sundays) with spiritual discipline and self-denial,

Holy Week with Maundy Thursday and Good Friday;

Easter, Resurrection, 50 days, remembered annually and

weekly;

Ascension,our risen Lord's return to heaven; and

Pentecost, the coming of the Holy Spirit.

Our worship carries with it *symbols* of colors, acts, garments, and

images. For example, colors symbolize the seasons: white for

Christmas, Easter, and weddings, and feasts; red for Pentecost

and martyred saints; purple for Advent and Lent; black for Good

Friday; and green for Epiphany.

Symbolic acts include the *water* of Baptism that represents life,

cleansing, and refreshment; the *laying on of hands* in Baptism,

Confirmation, and ordination shows empowerment; and *imposing*

ashes exhibits penitence.

What do priests and deacons wear as they serve? Clergy wear vestments such as a cassock, a long black garment for service; an alb, a long white straight garment worn over a cassock for purity. A cincture or waist rope is worn with an alb. Vestments may include a surplice, a white gathered over-garment.

A long colored strip, a stole, is worn about the neck. A deacon wears the stole only over the left shoulder; a priest wears the stole around the shoulders.

Some images are symbols. The fish is an ancient image representing the parable of the net and the initial letters of the Greek phrase "Jesus Christ Son of God, Savior" that spell the Greek word for Christ: ICTHUS. The dove represents the Holy Spirit as well as peace. Chi Rho are the first letters of the Greek word for Christ: X = CHI (CH) and P = RHO (R). Other images include the Lamb of God or Agnus Dei (Mk 1.10) and the Alpha and Omega (Rev 1.8) representing the Lord God as the first and the last.

INSIGHT

We church members benefit, then, as inheritors of this Body of Christ. Because of God's gift of his son and because of efforts and even martyrdom of saints who have "gone before," we have, quite unmerited, this church: *The Body of Christ.*

REVIEW

We have considered The Episcopal Church in brief definition. We looked specifically at the priniciples of the Lambeth Quadrilateral. The chapter also has a glimpse at seasons and symbols of the church.

4   The Gift of the Book of Common Prayer

ASSIGNMENT

Read through the Table of Contents and Morning Prayer and Evening Prayer in the <u>Book of Common Prayer</u> (BCP). Look particularly at Morning Prayer, Rite One, pp. 37-60 and Rite Two, pp. 75-102. Look, too, at Evening Prayer, Rite One, pp. 61-73 and Rite Two, pp. 115-126.

PREVIEW

This session considers <u>The Book of Common Prayer</u> through its history, services, and features.

FOCUS HISTORY

<u>The Book of Common Prayer</u> has undergone several revisions from that of Thomas Cranmer in 1549. In this country 1789, 1892, 1928, and most recently, 1979 have seen revisions. Our current BCP uses contemporary English and is heavily grounded in <u>The Holy Bible.</u> For example, the Daily Office uses readings of the Old and New testaments.

FOCUS SERVICES

Four types of services appear in BCP: regular services, services

for special days, services for personal occasions, and Episcopal

services. The regular ones are Morning and Evening Prayer and the

Holy Eucharist. Special day services cover The Great Litany, Ash

Wednesday, and the days of Holy Week.

Personal occasions involve Baptism, Confirmation, Marriage,

Reconciliation, ministrations in sickness and at death, and Burial.

Episcopal services include ordinations of bishop, priest, and deacon,

new ministry, and consecration of a building.

FOCUS MORNING AND EVENING PRAYER

The services of Morning and Evening Prayer are ancient, going back

to times of OT synagogues. Hourly prayers had names of times of

the day, Matins, Laud, Prime, Vespers, and Compline, for example.

While the Holy Eucharist may be the principal Sunday service,

Morning and Evening Prayer remain as daily services in many places

providing a spiritual rhythm for life.

Both services in rites one and two have three main parts: first, opening sentences, confession, and absolution. Second, the Invitatory and Psalter offer praise and thanksgiving for forgiveness received. The Word of God or the lessons come next, each followed by a canticle. The Apostle's Creed follows the biblical instruction. The third part has prayers of petition and intercession. A blessing follows. Again, these beautiful services are in wide use.

FOCUS FEATURES

In addition to the services, many aids to worship and private devotion appear in BCP. There are rubrics or directions, collects, other prayers and thanksgivings, the Psalter, Catechism, historical documents, Table for finding Holy Days, the Lectionary as a three year cycle, and the Daily Office Lectionary (two year cycle). The emphases of BCP rely on the Scriptures. The Psalter, pp. 585-808, as well as MP and EP are made up of material from The Holy Bible.

INSIGHT

We may overlook some fine BCP features unless they are emphasized: the tables for finding Easter, pp. 880ff.; the daily lectionary (pp.934ff); and Prayers and Thanksgivings (pp. 810-841). Especially helpful to persons new to individual and group prayers are prayers in times of sickness (pp.458ff).

REVIEW

<u>The Book of Common Prayer</u> has always relied upon the Scriptures. It has been updated several times to reflect current language use. This work provides a storehouse of regular and special services, prayers, the Psalter, lectionaries, and tables. Our lives and our services are enriched by this valuable resource of The Episcopal Church.

5   The Gift of the Sacraments

ASSIGNMENT

Read Holy Baptism (BCP 298-314), Holy Eucharist: Rite Two
(BCP 354-366) and BCP 844-862 of the Catechism. Look
particularly for "grace" and the Holy Eucharist "benefits."

PREVIEW

This session looks at the sacraments of Holy Baptism and the Holy
Eucharist through definition, description, and service with particular
attention to the Real Presence.

FOCUS DEFINITIONS

How can we define "sacraments"?

> The sacraments are outward and visible signs of inward and spiritual *grace*, given by Christ as sure and certain means by which we receive that grace.

> What is *grace*?

> *Grace* is God's favor towards us, unearned and undeserved; by *grace* God forgives our sins, enlightens our minds, stirs our hearts, and strengthens our wills.

> **The two great sacraments given by Christ to his Church are *Holy Baptism and the Holy Eucharist (BCP 857-858).***

In addition to these two sacraments the Church practices five *sacramental rites: confirmation, ordination, holy matrimony, reconciliation of a penitent, and unction.*

FOCUS DESCRIPTION

What is baptism?

> Holy Baptism is the sacrament by which God adopts us as his children and makes us members of Christ's Body, the Church, and inheritors of the kingdom of God. . . .
>
> The outward and visible sign of Baptism is water, in which the person is baptized in the Name of the Father, and of the Son, and of the Holy Spirit. . . .
>
> The inward and spiritual grace in Baptism is union with Christ in his death and resurrection, birth into God's family the Church, forgiveness of sins, and life in the Holy Spirit (BCP 858).

"The Holy Eucharist is the sacrament commanded by Christ for the continual remembrance of his life, death, and resurrection, until his coming again" (BCP 859).

This sacrament is also called the Lord's Supper, Holy Communion, the Divine Liturgy, and the Great Offering. "The outward and visible sign in the Eucharist is bread and wine. . . . The inward and spiritual grace . . . is the Body and Blood of Christ given to his people and received by faith" (BCP 859).

The Real Presence

In receiving Holy Communion there is a moment we witness, that is, we feel and sense the presence of the living Christ just as he gives himself for each of us. We say "Amen" as we receive the host, the bread or bread wafer. We say "Amen" as we sip the wine that is the blood of Christ because that "Amen" completes the action of our willingness to witness and to be ourself a continuing part of this sacrifice.
The action of the Eucharist is without completion unless and until we utter "Amen." Our saying "Amen" does more. It is our statement that, as Raimon Panikkar says in his book <u>Christophany</u>, each of us continues God's incarnation and becomes the Word. This is the gift of God of his son to every one of us.This is also our celebrating the real presence.
A m e n .

FOCUS SERVICES

The officiant at Holy Baptism may be bishop, priest, or sometimes, deacon. In brief, after the liturgy, sponsors present candidates and the officiant examines them. If the candidate is an infant or a young child, parents and godparents respond for the candidate. The officiant's series of questions relate to renouncing Satan and accepting Jesus Christ as Lord and Savior.

The Baptismal Covenant is a statement of faith and commitment to the Christian way of life. The Baptism of repentance for the forgive- ness of sins, the anointing or Christening, and the reception into the community of the faithful follow. The congregation acts as witness in support of this baptismal action.

The celebrant of the Holy Eucharist may be bishop or priest. The Greek words eucharistia, thanksgiving, and euchoristeuomen, let us give thanks, indicate the action. The celebration has two parts: The Liturgy and the Holy Communion.

The *Liturgy* contains opening rites of procession, greeting, Collect for Purity, and hymn of praise; Propers with collect, first lesson, psalm or hymn, second lesson, gradual, gospel, the sermon, the Nicene Creed, the Prayers of the People, the confession with invitation and absolution, and the exchange of the Peace.

The *Holy Communion* has the Offertory; the Great Thanksgiving with Sursum Corda or lifting of hearts, Proper Preface, Sanctus and Benedictus, Prayer of Consecration, and the Lord's Prayer; the Breaking of Bread with the Fraction, Fraction Anthem, Presentation of Gifts, and the distribution of communion; and Concluding Rites.

INSIGHT

Baptism operates as our "indissoluble" bond with God. The bond or covenant allows us to worship, to pray, to resist evil, to proclaim by word and deed the **"Good News of God in Christ"** as well as to **"seek and serve Christ in all persons"** (BCP 305).

The Holy Eucharist lets us act out and renew our baptismal vows. In Communion we offer thanks and gifts to God for God's gifts to us!

REVIEW

Both Baptism and the Holy Eucharist are outward, visible signs of Christ's inward, spiritual grace. In them we are made members of God's New Covenant community with its disciplines and responsibilities.

6

The Gift of Gathering

ASSIGNMENT

Reflect upon our gathering, our coming together as a parish family.

Consider questions of our worship, our teaching, our serving.

PREVIEW

We consider gathering in its meaning and ministry.

FOCUS MEANING

What is *gathering* ? For most of us our parish is our church. While

dioceses and provinces function within the national community, we

know the Episcopal Church most regularly in this local family

community of our gathering.

Effective *gathering* of the Body of Christ in worship requires a central point. That center or **focus** may be altar, Christ figure, liturgy, Holy Eucharist, or all of these functioning as **focus** as we have **interaction** with each other in God's presence.

The more active our multi-sensational intermingling in worship, the better is our communicating the GOOD NEWS. Our **focus** and **interaction** with our mingling produce **group memory.**

As example, in entering the nave of Saint Nicholas Episcopal Church in Pompano Beach, Florida, we face eastward. Ahead is our communion rail. Inside the rail is a white marble altar, our Lord's table; above this Holy Table is our **focus,** a larger than life-size figure of Jesus Christ in Majesty.

Our liturgy and the Holy Communion center there, and we share **interaction** as we respond corporately in our loving worship of God, mingle in exchanging the peace, and produce **group memory** in praying for individuals and in celebrating the Holy Eucharist.

FOCUS CORPORATE WORSHIP

It is important to explain corporate worship. What is it? As we believers worship God each day or each Sunday in a church building, our action is corporate. Corporate worship demands our ready participation in all parts of all services.

"In corporate worship, we unite ourselves with others to acknowledge the holiness of God, to hear God's Word, to offer prayer, and to celebrate the sacraments" (BCP 857). We unite as Christ's Body; we worship as an individual to give hearty praise and thanks to God.

FOCUS MINISTRY

Our intentions in gathering besides sharing our worship include reaching out to the unchurched with food, clothing, education. Another intention is to celebrate the joy of our *being.* A further intention is our *believing* we are the Body of Christ. Besides our *being and believing,* we can be active, as John Westerhoff says, in *behaving* as the Body of Christ (91). Many ministries are avenues to **be, believe, and behave as Christ's Body.**

Acolytes- 3rd graders and older who serve at the altar

Altar Guild- members prepare altar, care for linens, vestments, flowers . . . .*

Bible Study

Book or gift shop

Boy Scouts- local troop

Chalicers- serve at altar, assist in administering chalice

Choir

Christian Education Teachers- provide classes for all age levels

Crucifers- carry the cross; serve at altar

Cursillo- little course in Christianity; interested persons meet some weekends and in small groups for study, friendship

Daughters of the King- (DOK) women dedicated to prayer and service

Episcopal Church Women- (ECW) all females of parish, service and friendship

Episcopal Young Churchmen- males and females of high school and college age, service and friendship

Episcopal School- parish day education, pre-kindergarten through 8th grade or high school

Eucharistic Visitors- (formerly Lay Eucharistic Ministers) General Convention name change since 2003. These are trained persons who provide Holy Communion for hospitalized and homebound

Finance Commission- persons responsible for pledges

Girl Scouts- local troop

Greeters- persons who arrive early to meet worshippers before parish activities

Intercessors-lead prayers for others during services

Lectors- read lessons at services

Long Range Planning Commission- interested persons looking ahead to parish needs . . .

Men's Club- all males of parish, service and fellowship

Mission for the Deaf- interested persons provide services of sign language, interpreting . . .

Outreach Commision- persons responsible for our contributing to needs in the local area

Prayer Chain- persons who intercede for needs of individuals

Stewardship Commission- persons coordinating our individual uses of gifts of minutes, minds, and monies

Thrift Shop- collects goods from parishioners and sells for nominal amounts . . .

Transporters- provide needed rides

Ushers- provide order, distribute programs, take offering during services, and make certain pews are left clean and in order

Vestry-elected persons who meet regularly overseeing parish operation

Visitors- call on homebound

★ **The ellipsis suggests much more done in this ministry than can be explained in a one or two line blurb.**

INSIGHT

In our gathering as Christian family, our parish affords us opportunities in our baptismal mission to seek and serve. Here we look for Jesus Christ in those we meet. Here we also work for Christ in tending to needs of parishioners.

REVIEW

Our gathering relies upon our regular worship, continuing education, and active ministry in caring for each other. Our focusing on Jesus Christ and the altar allows us to say "thank you" to God in our words, music, and actions. We can **be the Body of Christ, believe in the Body of Christ, and behave as the Body of Christ.**

ACTIVITIES

Invite the senior and/or junior warden to tell the group what part the the vestry plays in the gathering of the parish. What occurs at a regular meeting?

Invite the director or a teacher from the church school to describe the program and encourage volunteers.

7
The Gift of Life

ASSIGNMENT

Rom 6: 23   1 Cor 12: 1, 8-11

Eph 2: 8   2 Cor 9: 7-15

1 Pet 4: 10-11   1 Tim 4: 14

Rom 12: 6-8   BCP 855-857

Pray for the worship, the study, the prayer, and the ministry of each

of us in our lives in Christ in our parish.

PREVIEW

This session considers the gift of life, our worship, our study, our

prayer and our lay ministry in using this overwhelming gift.

FOCUS   WORSHIP

"The ministers of the Church are lay persons, bishops, priests, and deacons" (BCP 855). "The duty of all Christians is to follow Christ; to come together week by week for corporate worship; and to work, pray, and give for the spread of the kingdom of God" (BCP 856).

FOCUS   STUDY

If we are "to hear . . . read, mark, learn, and inwardly digest" Holy Scriptures (BCP 236), we need to study the Holy Bible with regularity. In order to do that we need to approach the task with prayer, with expectance that we gain from what we read, and with obedience. Helps are available for finding our way: a concordance that lists words and their occurrences in the Bible and the Interpreter's Bible, one or multivolume, are but two among hundreds of aids. The Oxford Companion to the Bible offers excellent help, too.

We may benefit from group study; we may find we gain in reading alone. Whatever approach we choose, it is vital to have a plan for each day. Regular reading of MP and EP gives structure and purpose to our days. Following some procedure benefits us most in gaining discipline in Christian maturity or order to build up the Body of Christ.

FOCUS   PRAYER

New Covenant prayer is that unique time and place in God's presence where we join Jesus most consciously in his still to be completed work of whole created order. We are indebted to John Koenig, author of <u>Rediscovering New Testament Prayer</u>, for this definition.

As an example, we give thanks in prayer as we embrace the gift of life God has given you and me. This great gift **of life** is placed last here because we are ordinarily *slow to recognize its worth.*

We pray for any number of reasons - - - to give *praise* for being in God's presence, to *give thanks* to God for each part of this day, to *intercede* for needs of others, to *petition* for help for ourselves, as a means of *penitence*. We also pray to offer ourselves for God's purposes. We pray for God's will, not ours.

Simply saying "Abba, Father," a prayer in itself, acknowledges and allows God to work his will in us. We need to pray with honesty as the man in Mark 9. 21-24 who asks that Jesus help his "unbelief." We need especially to pray with perseverence. Walter Wink says that we pray the future into being.

Once we pray for anything we need to proceed as though we had been answered. We need to take care in what we pray for because when we get it, we may no longer want it. We particularly need to pray for discernment to be able to recognize our own gifts and their potential use. We do, indeed, become what we pray.

FOCUS   LAY MINISTRY

We have not only the gift of **life** but also the gift of earth on which to live it. We have, in effect, a time-share arrangement with God in our use of the earth. As stewards, managers, tenders of that life, what do we do with this trust? Asked another way, "What ought I to offer as my lay ministry?"

Can I teach, heal, serve, prophesy, exhort, discern, listen, or speak wisely? Discerning our abilities comes through dialog with God. When we ask, "Lord, what would you have me do?," an answer is sure to come.

We act out our thanksgiving to God for what we have by offering our mind, minutes, and money to serve him. We offer clothing, equipment, food, furniture, and possessions for the use of others. We distinctively offer our abilities, skills, gifts, talents for God's use.

Here begins an alphabet "primer"; its intent is to elicit further thoughts and actions:

ADORATION   AFFIRMATION   ART

BEFRIENDING   BLOOD   BOUNTY

CARE   CHEER   CLEANING   CONSTANCY

CALM   CREATIVITY

DESIGN   DEVOTION

ENCOURAGEMENT   ENTHUSIASM

FAITH   FONDNESS   FOOD   FRIENDSHIP

GIVING   GLEE   GRAPHICS   GROCERIES

HEALTH   HEART   HONOR

INTEGRITY   INTEREST   IRONING

JOY

KNOWLEDGE

LAUNDERING   LISTENING   LOVE

MEDICINE   MIND   MINUTES   MONEY   MUSIC

NEARNESS   NURSING   NURTURE

OBLATION   OPENNESS   ORGAN

PLEDGE   PRAYER   PROFESSION

QUIET

READING   RENEWAL   RISK-TAKING   ROOFING

SERVICE   SILENCE   SOUL   SHELTER   STUDY

TEACHING   TIME   TITHE   TOLERANCE

 TRANSPORTATION

UNDERSTANDING

VENERATION   VISIT   VOICE (ALTO   BASS   SOPRANO

 TENOR)

WELCOME   WORK

XEROXING

YOUTH

ZEAL

Almighty God, whose loving hand has given us all that we possess: Grant us grace that we may honor you with our substance, and, remembering the account which we must one day give, grant that we may be faithful stewards of your bounty, through Jesus Christ our Lord. Amen (adaption BCP 827).

INSIGHT

Kinds of prayer include adoration, praise, thanksgiving, penitence, oblation, intercession, and petition. We may begin begging for ourselves; a response to our plea prompts our expressions of gratitude. As followers of Christ we may find we start in adoration and soon spill over into other acts of prayer. Yesterday's petitions do become the bases of today's praise, action, and thanks.

God gives us through his grace, then, our life, the scriptures, the Body of Christ, sacraments, prayer book, and gathering. What may we do with these *Gifts of God*? Much as he calls Abraham, Moses, David, and the apostles, God calls you and me through our Baptismal Covenant to respond to these loving gifts.

When God calls us to act, he supplies us with skills needed for that act. Hearing his call seems a first step. We can pursue that hearing by answering his call(s), praying for guidance, and, with God's help, acting for him. Amen.

REVIEW

We have considered briefly the gift of life. The call to worship regularly, study diligently, pray perseveringly, and serve obediently is part of this life. Amen.

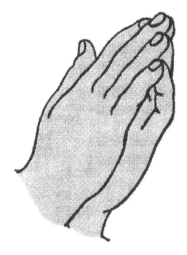

The Gifts of God for the People of God. Take them in remembrance that Christ died for you, and feed on him in your hearts by faith, with thanksgiving. Amen (BCP 338).

APPENDIX A-- GETTING STARTED

This course requires eight one-hour sessions. Sunday morning education periods seem productive times. As class members arrive for the first session, each completes a 4 X 6" card with name, address, telephone number and best time to call, church status (baptized, confirmed), and preferred first name. When all have arrived, the teacher leads the group in opening prayer (Appendix B).

The teacher places the collected cards in front of him or her to correspond to the seating arrangement of that day. In this way the teacher can address each person by name. The cards are placed according to seating for succeeding sessions until individual names are well known. (Telephone numbers permit the teacher to follow up in case of absence.)

Paired interviews provide an exercise in listening and allow getting acquainted. Class members in pairs interview each other for about three minutes each. Then the teacher calls on each to present to the group the person just interviewed until all are presented.

The teacher then distributes Gifts of God booklets (and bibles if they are given) and briefly explains format and assignments. The bible reading assignments allow home preparation as well as full class participation as individuals read passages aloud in session for discussion. The teacher asks members to bring bibles and booklets for the next session.

Various biblical translations invite a welcome diversity for comparison in Revised Standard Version (RSV), New Revised Standard Version (NRSV), New English Bible (NEB), Revised English Bible (REB), New International Version (NIV), and American Standard Version (ASV). The teacher assigns the reading of the first chapter for the next session with its assignment. The session ends with closing prayer (Appendix B).

Note: Many diocesan offices provide helpful aids such as the twenty minute video produced by Episcopal Radio TV Foundation: Baptism: Sacrament of New Birth (no date given).

APPENDIX B

PRAYERS

SESSION

1	Getting started	BCP 261 #23,#24
2	Old Testament	BCP 236 #28
3	New Testament	BCP 236 #28
4	The Body of Christ	BCP 255 #14
5	The Book of Common Prayer	*
6	Sacraments	BCP 252 # 5, BCP 254 # 10
7	Gathering	BCP 254-255 # 12
8	Life	BCP 259 # III

*   Almighty God, who has given us every good gift, accept our gratitude for The Book of Common Prayer. Through it we worship you and are guided in our devotions. Its words lift us up and express what we may be unable to say. We thank you for inspiring its writers and for encouraging us in its use. We ask this in the name of Jesus Christ our Lord. Amen (Prayer written expressly for Session 5 on BCP).

APPENDIX B PRAYERS

CLOSING PRAYER

Holy Lord: Your mighty works reveal your wisdom and love. You formed us in your image, giving the whole world into our care. Again and again you called us into covenant with you. We ask that we may be open to hear your call so that we may know what you would have us do, through Jesus Christ our Lord. Amen.
(Adapted from BCP 373)

APPENDIX C

MAJOR EVENTS IN OLD TESTAMENT HISTORY

Approximate Date B.C.E	Event	Biblical source
About 1850	Abraham leaves northern Mesopotamia & journeys to Canaan	Gen. 12
About 1280- 1250	Moses leads the Israelites out of Egypt to Mt. Sinai	Exod. 13-15
Following 1250	Joshua leads conquest of Canaan	Josh. 1-24
About 1200-1030	Israel is loosely knit 12-tribe confederacy; period of the judges	Judg. 1-21
About 1020	Samuel anoints Saul king of Israel over 12-tribe kingdom	1 Sam. 10
About 1000-961	David creates Israelite Empire; makes Jerusalem national capital	2 Sam 2-21; 1 Kings 2
About 961-922	King Solomon rules: builds temple at Jerusalem	1 Kings 3-11
922	Kingdom split into 10-tribe northern state (Israel) and 2-tribe southern	1 Kings 12

	state (Judah)	
721	Assyria conquers Israel, destroys its capital, Samaria; deports its population	2 Kings 17
701	Sennacherib besieges Jerusalem; Assyrians withdraw	Isa. 36-37; 2 Kings 18-19

APPENDIX C

621	Book of Deuteronomy "discovered"; Josiah reforms Judah's religion	2 Kings 22-23; 2 Chron. 34-35
598/597	Nebuchadnezzar sacks Jerusalem; first deporta- tion of Jewish captives	
587	Nebuchadnezzar destroys Jerusalem, burns Solomon's Temple, takes Jews captive to Babylon	2 Kings 24
539	Cyrus the Great of Persia captures Babylon	
538	Jewish remnant returns to Jerusalem	Ezra 1
520-515	Second Temple built & dedicated Judah becomes province of Persian Empire	Ezra 6 Hag. 2
445ff.	Ezra and Nehemiah: religious reforms; the Torah is promulgated	Neh. 8
About 332	Alexander the Great of Macedonia includes Palestine in his empire	1 Macc. 1
323-197	The Ptolemys of Egypt rule Palestine (Hellenistic period)	

APPENDIX C

197-142	Seleucid dynasty of Syria rules Palestine	2 Macc. 4
167-164	Antiochus IV attempts to force religion Jews; pollutes Temple	1 Macc.; Dan. 11:30
164	The Maccabeaan revolt successsful; Temple is cleaned & rededicated	Dan. 7:25; 12:7; 8:14; 9:27
142-63	The Jews expel the Seleucids; Judea becomes independent kingdom under Hasmonean dynasty	1 Macc.
63	General Pompey makes Palestine part of Roman Empire; partitions Judea	
66-73 C.E.	The Jews revolt against Rome	
70 C.E.	The Romans destroy Jerusalem and the Temple	
90-91 C.E.	Jewish rabbis assemble at Jamnia to formulate biblical canon	

Harris, Stephen L. Understanding the Bible. 3rd ed. London: Mayfield, 1992.

APPENDIX D

ENGLISH TRANSLATIONS OF THE BIBLE

c. 670   Anglo-saxon paraphrases of narratives of Caedmon

c. 735   Gospel of John translated into Anglo-Saxon by Bede

c. 900   Exodus, Acts, Psalms translated by King Alfred

1530   William Tyndale's Pentateuch

1534   Martin Luther's Old Testament

1535   Miles Coverdale's Bible

1560   Geneva Bible (Shakespeare's Bible)

1611   King James Version- Authorized

1717   Vinegar Bible*

1901   American Standard Version (RC)

1952   Revised Standard Version (American, Protestant)

APPENDIX D CONTINUED

1966   Jerusalem Bible   (translated from French, RC)

1970   New English Bible   (British, Protestant)

1978   New International Version

1982   New American Jewish Version

        New King James Version

1986   Revised English bible

1990   New Revised Standard Version

Other revisions are in process; watch for their publication.

★ **A printer setting the type consistently misrepresented "vineyard" as "vinegar." The so called Vinegar Bible resulted.**

APPENDIX   SYMBOLS

ICTHUS

CHI RHO

DOVE

APPENDIX F   PROVINCES OF THE

EPISCOPAL CHURCH

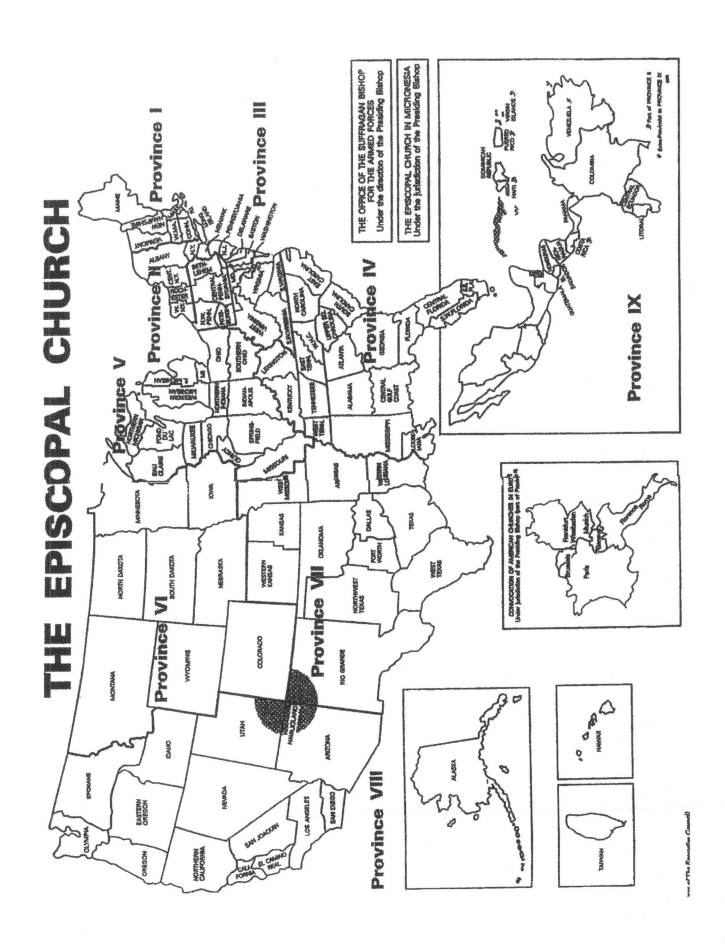

THE EPISCOPAL CHURCH

APPENDIX G

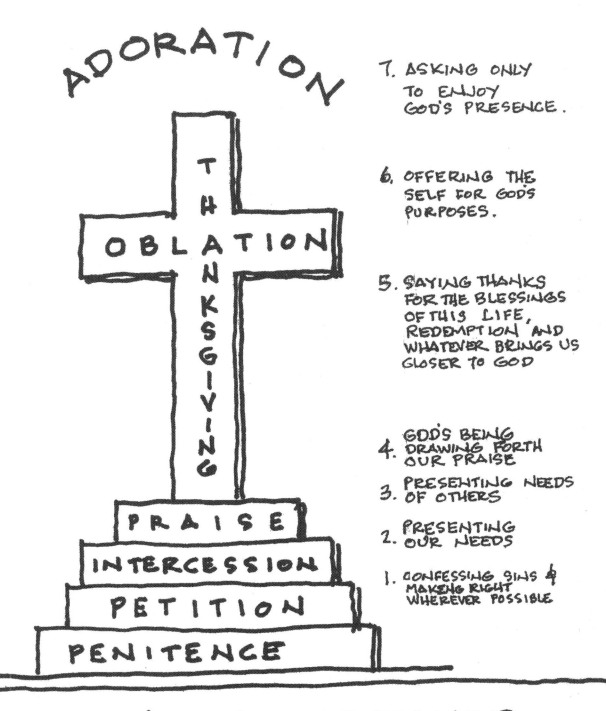

ADORATION

OBLATION

THANKSGIVING

PRAISE

INTERCESSION

PETITION

PENITENCE

7. ASKING ONLY TO ENJOY GOD'S PRESENCE.

6. OFFERING THE SELF FOR GOD'S PURPOSES.

5. SAYING THANKS FOR THE BLESSINGS OF THIS LIFE, REDEMPTION AND WHATEVER BRINGS US CLOSER TO GOD

4. GOD'S BEING DRAWING FORTH OUR PRAISE

3. PRESENTING NEEDS OF OTHERS

2. PRESENTING OUR NEEDS

1. CONFESSING SINS & MAKING RIGHT WHEREVER POSSIBLE

SEVEN KINDS OF PRAYER

BOOK OF COMMON PRAYER
CATECHISM   PP 856-7
PSWIFT: ANDREW APRIL 2002

BIBLIOGRAPHY

Armentrout, Don S., and Robert Boak Slocum, eds. An Episcopal Dictionary of the Church A User Friendly Reference for Episcopalians. New York: Church Publishing Incorporated, n.d.

The Book of Common Prayer and Administration of the Sacraments And Other Rites and Ceremonies of the Church Together With The Psalter or Psalms of David According to the use of the Episcopal Church. New York: The Church Hymnal Corp., 1979.

Capon, Robert Farrar. The Parables of Grace. Grand Rapids, MI: Eerdman's, 1988.

------ The Parables of Judgement. Grand Rapids, MI: Eerdman's, 1989.

-----The Parables of the Kingdom. Grand Rapids, MI: Eerdman's, 1985.

Harris, Stephen L. Understanding the Bible. 3rd ed. London: Mayfield, 1992.

Hoag, Victor. A Chart of Church History Showing Church History as a River Updated 1999. Rev. William L. Sachs. Harrisburg, PA: Morehouse Publishing, 1999.

Koenig, John. Rediscovering New Testament Prayer Boldness and Blessing in the Name of Jesus. San Francisco: Harper, 1992.

Meeks, Wayne A., et al., eds. The HarperCollins Study Bible New Revised Standard Version with Apocrypha/Deuterocanonical Books. New York: HarperCollins, 1993.

Metzger, Bruce M., and Michael D. Coogan, eds. The Oxford Companion to the Bible. New York: Oxford UP, 1993.

Panikkar, Raimon. Christophany. Trans. Alfred DiLascra. Maryknoll, NY: Orbis, 2004.

Ramsey, Michael. The Anglican Spirit. Ed. Dale D. Coleman. New York: Church Pub. Inc., 2004.

Sydnor, William. Looking at the Episcopal Church. Wilton, CT:

Morehouse-Barlow, 1980.

Westerhoff III, John H. Living the Faith Community. New York:

Church Pub. Inc., 2004.

Wright, G. Ernest. "The Theological Study of the Bible." The

Interpreter's One Volume Commentary on the Bible. Ed.

Charles M. Laymon. Nashville: Abingdon, 1971.

Afterword

Late Autumn of 1993 Father Ralph Evans asked me to write down what a newcomer to the Episcopal Church needs to know. Reflection on what we have and what we lack resulted in this catechumenate. Looking again at this material I see it as my own confession of faith. This booklet has these aims for the reader: regular reading of the Holy Bible, full use of individual abilities and continual thanksgiving in praise-filled prayer. Gifts of God serves as an introduction to the Episcopal Church, preparation for confirmands and those to be received, affirmation for those who would renew their faith. I pray for the reader's full realization of the Gifts of God.

The writer expresses gratitude to the Reverend Michael F. Gray and the Reverend Timothy B. Thomas for their guidance.